Fact Finders®

THE
INVENTION
OF THE
TELEVISION

by Lucy Beevor

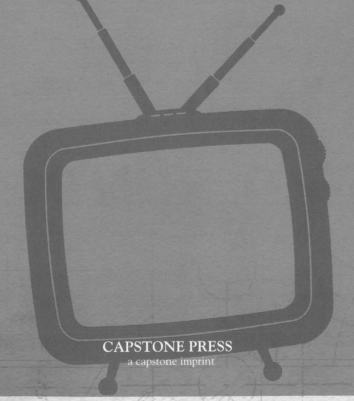

CAPSTONE PRESS
a capstone imprint

Fact Finders Books are published by Capstone Press,
1710 Roe Crest Drive, North Mankato, Minnesota 56003
www.mycapstone.com

Library of Congress Cataloging-in-Publication Data
Cataloging-in-publication information is on file with the Library of Congress.
ISBN 978-1-5157-9844-6 (library binding)
ISBN 978-1-5157-9852-1 (paperback)
ISBN 978-1-5157-9860-6 (eBook PDF)

Editorial Credits
Jennifer Huston, editor; Heidi Thompson, designer; Eric Gohl, media researcher;
Katy LaVigne, production specialist

Photo Credits
Alamy: Dennis MacDonald, 23, Everett Collection Historical, 16, 17, INTERFOTO, 19 (bottom),
Science History Images, 6, 11, World History Archive, 8; Getty Images: Bettmann, 15; iStockphoto:
jack0m, 21; NASA: 4, 5; Newscom: EFE/Miguel Gutierrez, 22, Everett Collection, 7, Mirrorpix, 9,
Oronoz/Album, 13; Shutterstock: 360b, 24 (television screen), Aleks49, cover (bottom right),
Aleksandr Bryliaev, 1, Andrey_Popov, 26, BrAt82, cover (top right), Dmitry Naumov, cover
(top middle), Everett Collection, 19 (top), Farhad Bek, cover (bottom middle), 2, Gino Santa Maria,
cover (top left), jakkapan, cover (bottom left), Monkey Business Images, 24, 27, Perfect Vectors,
20, Scanrail1, 25, SergeyPhoto7, 14

Design Elements: Shutterstock

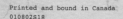
Printed and bound in Canada
010802S18

TABLE OF CONTENTS

THE FIRST MAN ON THE MOON

On July 20, 1969, millions of people around the world tuned in to watch the astronauts of the *Apollo 11* mission land on the moon. Commander Neil Armstrong was the first man to step onto the moon's surface. Buzz Aldrin followed a few minutes later. When the astronauts returned home on July 24, they were welcomed as international heroes. The *Apollo 11* mission was a major success.

As Neil Armstrong set foot on the moon, he said the now famous words, "That's one small step for man, one giant leap for mankind."

The moon landing was filmed and **broadcast** around the world. The broadcast set a new world record, as more than half a billion people tuned in to watch the historic event. Even today, that's a lot of people watching one television show.

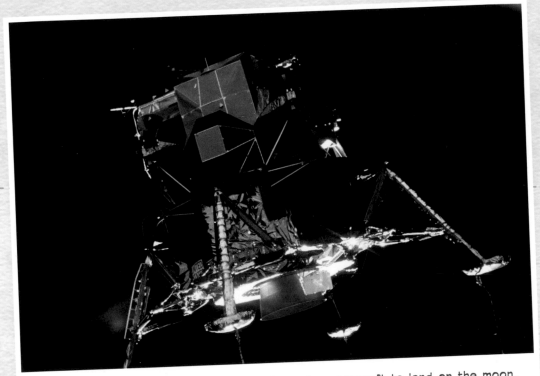

The *Eagle* lunar module detached from the main spacecraft to land on the moon.

BEFORE TELEVISION

Before television was invented, people entertained themselves in other ways. Families sat around the fireplace and told stories. They also read books, sang songs, and played instruments. They played card games and board games, such as chess and backgammon. Children also played with wooden toys. In the 1700s and 1800s, a favorite children's game was hoop rolling.

In hoop rolling, the player tries to roll the hoop along the ground by hitting it with a stick.

THE RADIO IS INVENTED

By the late 1800s, the world was changing. People used more machines. The radio was invented in 1895, but for the first 25 years, it was mainly used for sending **wireless messages**. Then on August 31, 1920, the first radio news program was broadcast in Detroit, Michigan. In the UK, the British Broadcasting Corporation (BBC) began broadcasting radio shows every day starting in 1922. The shows included music, news, and other entertainment. Listening to the radio quickly became very popular.

Before television, people listened to the radio for news and entertainment.

wireless message—a telegraph message sent over a long distance using radio waves instead of wires

THE FIRST MOVIES

In the mid-1890s, movies were also invented. These moving pictures amazed people. At first, the movies showed pictures without sound. They were called "silent movies." Musicians played live music to go along with the moving pictures.

In 1927, *The Jazz Singer* became the first successful full-length movie with sound. People called movies with sound "talkies."

CHARLIE CHAPLIN

Charlie Chaplin was one of the first movie stars. He appeared in many famous silent movies, including *The Kid* (1921) and *The Circus* (1928).

Charlie Chaplin was a star of the silent-movie era.

technology—the use of science to do practical things, such as designing complex machines

MECHANICAL TELEVISION

The mechanical television was an early idea for sending moving pictures over long distances. In London, England, in 1926, John Logie Baird of Scotland showed the mechanical television he'd invented. It used a spinning disk that copied a picture line by line. Then each line was sent to another disk. That disk put the image back together.

In 1927, Baird formed the Baird Television Development Company (BTDC). In 1928 the BTDC became the first company to send televised pictures across the Atlantic Ocean between London and New York. The first mechanical TVs went on sale later that year.

John Logie Baird in his workshop

The BBC began broadcasting pictures using Baird's mechanical system. But it was slow, plus the pictures were fuzzy, and they fluttered on the screen. Even so, Baird's work was an important step in the development of television. **Technology** was changing rapidly, and someone needed to find a way to make clearer, faster pictures.

3 > INVENTORS OF TELEVISION

People soon realized that if picture quality was going to improve, televisions would need to be electronic. Philo T. Farnsworth and Vladimir Zworykin were two early inventors of the electronic television. Their work led to the televisions we watch today.

PHILO T. FARNSWORTH

Philo T. Farnsworth was an American electrical **engineer**. When Farnsworth was just 14 years old, he came up with the idea to use electricity to send pictures. Like Baird's mechanical system, Farnsworth's system divided the picture into lines. However, there was one big difference. Instead of spinning disks, Farnsworth believed that he could turn the lines into radio **signals**. The signals could be sent from one place to another using electricity. Then the lines could be put back together to form a picture.

In 1927, Farnsworth filed a **patent** for a camera tube called the image dissector. It was an early version of a television camera. The image dissector could change a picture into a radio signal. That same year, Farnsworth sent the first electronic television picture from the image dissector to a screen in another room in his lab. The picture was a straight line he had painted on a piece of glass.

He lit the picture from behind with a bright lamp. The following year, Farnsworth showed his system to the media by sending a picture of a dollar sign. It was the first working all-electronic television system.

Farnsworth holds his image dissector while standing next to his television. He received a patent for the image dissector in 1930.

engineer—one who uses science and math to design and build things
signal—a radio, sound, or light wave that sends information from one place to another
patent—a legal document giving sole rights to make or sell a product

VLADIMIR ZWORYKIN

Vladimir Zworykin was an electrical engineer from Russia. He moved to the United States in 1919. Zworykin was working on his own version of an all-electronic television system around the same time as Farnsworth. Zworykin called his system the iconoscope, and he applied for a patent for it in 1923. Similar to Farnsworth's image dissector, the iconoscope could also change a picture into a radio signal. But Zworykin struggled to make the iconoscope work. Finally, in 1933, he was able to send a picture with the iconoscope. Zworykin received a patent for it in 1938.

Vladimir Zworykin holds an iconoscope.

DID YOU KNOW?

Early inventors used different names for the television. Some of these names were radiovision, radiovisor, and televisor.

While he worked on the iconoscope, Zworykin invented a picture tube in 1929. He called it the kinescope. The kinescope was an early television **receiver**—a **vacuum tube** that could receive radio signals. It changed the radio signals back into pictures.

Today, a monument showing Zworykin and his television is on display in Moscow, Russia.

receiver—a device that receives radio signals and turns them into sound or pictures
vacuum tube—a glass tube that was used in the past in computers and televisions to control the flow of electricity

LEGAL PROBLEMS

All of these inventions led to the creation of television as we know it today. But the race to make the first working system led to legal problems for Zworykin and Farnsworth. Zworykin worked for the Radio Corporation of America (RCA). RCA offered Farnsworth $100,000 for the patent to the image dissector, but Farnsworth refused. So RCA took Farnsworth to court. RCA tried to say that because Zworykin filed his patent first, Farnsworth's shouldn't be legal. When the legal battles ended in 1939, the court ruled that RCA could sell electronic TVs for home use. But RCA had to pay Farnsworth $1 million for the rights to make the necessary television parts he'd invented.

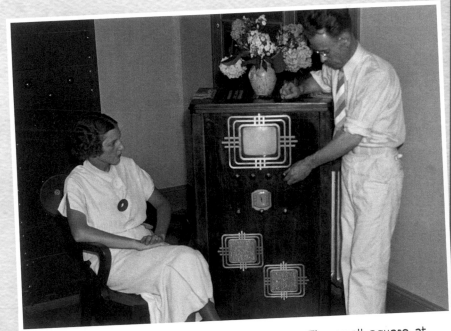

Farnsworth shows one of his early televisions. The small square at the top is where the picture was shown.

THE FIRST TELEVISION PROGRAMS

4

Over time Farnsworth and Zworykin's inventions became popular. But it didn't happen overnight. In the 1930s the first television broadcasts in the United States were fuzzy pictures of dancing and wrestling. Few people even saw those broadcasts because the number of television stations was limited. The number of people who owned televisions was even fewer.

Many new inventions were displayed at the New York World's Fair in 1939.

variety show—a show with many different types of performers, such as dancers, singers, and comedians

16

Many people in the United States saw television for the first time at the 1939 World's Fair in New York. American companies such as General Electric, Westinghouse Electric, and RCA showed televisions at the fair. The National Broadcasting Company (NBC) began TV broadcasts on April 30, the opening day of the World's Fair. That same year, NBC was the first network to show a baseball game on TV. NBC also broadcast cartoons, game shows, cooking shows, and **variety shows**.

People crowded around the television on display at the 1939 World's Fair in New York.

The first black-and-white electronic televisions went on sale in Germany in 1934, followed by the UK in 1936, and the United States in 1938. The first TVs sold for $200 to $600 (about £150 to £450). At the same time, the first TV stations formed. But during World War II (1939–1945), manufacturing of televisions stopped, and it wasn't until after the war that TV became really popular.

NEW FEATURES

By the 1950s, televisions had many new features. The first remote control was available in 1950. The earliest remote controls were attached to the television by a wire. The first wireless remote control came out in 1956. Color TVs went on sale in 1953.

CLOSED-CAPTIONING

Closed-captioning is a feature that prints spoken words across a television screen. It was first developed so that hearing-impaired people could enjoy TV programs. The first closed-captioning system was displayed at the 1971 National Conference on Television for the Hearing Impaired in Knoxville, Tennessee. After several more years of tests and the invention of machines to write the captions, closed-captioning was finally made available on all U.S. TV channels in 1980.

CHANGING STYLES

Television styles have changed over the years. Early TVs had small screens, and their parts were tucked inside large wooden frames. By the 1970s and 1980s, TVs were built with more plastic. They had rounded screens and came in many shapes and sizes.

Many televisions in the 1950s came in large wooden cabinets.

In the 1960s and 1970s, plastic TVs came in all shapes, sizes, and colors.

HOW ANALOG TELEVISIONS WORKED

Before the 2000s, televisions were **analog**.
Broadcasting stations sent out picture and
sound signals. Televisions created pictures
and sounds from the signals they received.
Picture signals went to the TV screen. Sound
signals went to the speakers.

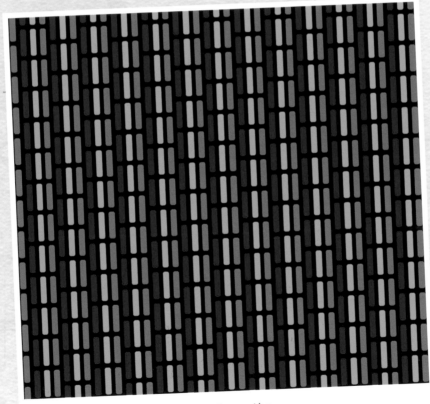

Blue, green, and red dots made up the
pictures on an analog color TV.

CATHODE-RAY TUBES

Analog TVs used a cathode, an anode, and a screen to show pictures. These parts made up a cathode-ray tube. A cathode is a heated wire that releases electrons, one of the tiny pieces of an atom. An anode focuses the electrons into a beam. The beam of electrons is shot at the screen, which is coated with phosphor. Phosphor is a material that glows when electrons hit it.

The pictures on an analog TV screen were made up of dots and lines. The electron beam drew each picture dot by dot, line by line.

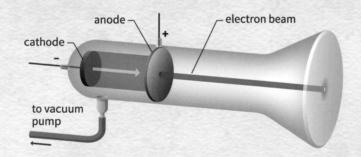

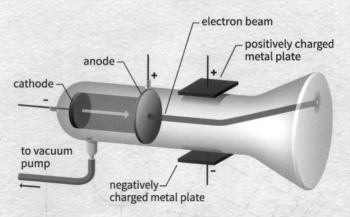

analog—the opposite of digital; pictures on an analog TV are made from dots and lines

5

TELEVISION TODAY

New technology in the 2000s made **digital** televisions possible. Today, most televisions are digital. In the United States, broadcasting stations began using digital signals on June 12, 2009.

With digital TV, you can choose from hundreds of channels.

A BETTER PICTURE

Digital television uses a digital signal to send pictures and sound. A digital signal is made up of a series of 0s and 1s. This **data** takes up much less space than analog signals. More space allows for clearer pictures and sound. It also allows for more features, such as program descriptions, sound in different languages, and special services for visually- and hearing-impaired people.

Digital TVs also have space for many more channels. Analog TVs in the United States had a limited number of channels. Digital TVs have hundreds of channels.

Closed-captioning helps hearing-impaired people read what is being said during a television program.

digital—the opposite of analog; using binary numbers (0s and 1s) in a form that can be used on a computer or television

data—information or facts

23

HIGH-DEFINITION TVS

Companies now make high-definition televisions (HDTVs) to receive digital signals. HDTVs have wide and flat screens. Wider screens give people the feeling that they are watching a movie screen.

Wide screens can also be larger. In 2014, Samsung launched the largest home TV with a 110-inch (279-centimeter) screen. It cost $150,000! Most people can't afford a screen that large, but many have 40- or 50-inch (102- or 127-centimeter) or even larger flat screens in their homes.

HDTVs have wide screens. Many are thin enough to hang on a wall.

SHARPER PICTURES

HDTVs do not use cathode-ray tubes. Instead, they use liquid crystal displays (LCDs) and plasma displays. LCDs pass light through liquid crystals to form images. Plasma displays pass an electric current through a gaslike material called plasma. The plasma shines light on phosphor to create pictures. LCD and plasma TVs create clearer pictures than TVs with cathode-ray tubes.

NEW TECHNOLOGY

TV technology is always changing and improving. Today, some companies make TVs with curved screens. This gives people the feeling that the picture wraps around them, making the viewer feel like he or she is part of the action.

People can also buy 4K TVs (ultra high-definition) and even 3D TVs. Not all TV programs are suitable for 4K or 3D viewing, but more and more are becoming available to viewers.

TELEVISION ON THE GO

The move from analog to digital television was the biggest change to television since color TV was invented in the 1950s. And technology is still changing rapidly. Today, viewers can **stream** television over the Internet. This allows people to watch TV on the go, wherever they can connect to the Internet. Viewers can stream hundreds of television shows and movies on computers, laptops, tablets, and even their smartphones.

Today, people can watch TV outside the home on their smartphones or tablets.

stream—to watch or listen to video or music at the same time that it is being downloaded to your device from the Internet

People can also download TV programs and movies. This means that they can save the program to their personal device and watch it without an Internet connection.

STAYING CONNECTED

Many people did not own a television 75 years ago. Since then, television has changed our lives. It entertains us. It delivers news. It lets people learn about each other. Television connects people around the world.

Television is one of the main ways people entertain themselves.

TELEVISION TODAY

Today, people watch TV programs on many different devices, including TVs, computers, smartphones, and tablets. This infographic shows that in a 24-hour day, the average person spends more than 10 hours on various electronic devices. More than 5 hours is spent watching television.

Total: 10 hours, 39 minutes

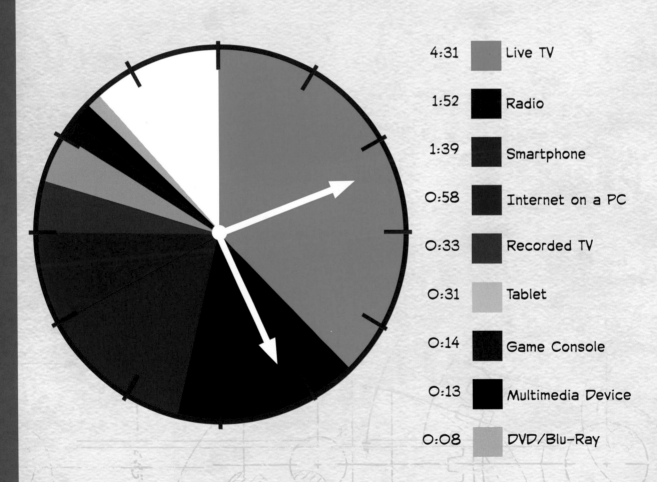

4:31	Live TV
1:52	Radio
1:39	Smartphone
0:58	Internet on a PC
0:33	Recorded TV
0:31	Tablet
0:14	Game Console
0:13	Multimedia Device
0:08	DVD/Blu-Ray

TIMELINE

1920	The first radio news program is broadcast in Detroit, Michigan
1922	The BBC begins broadcasting radio shows every day
1926	John Logie Baird builds the first mechanical television
1927	The first successful movie with sound, *The Jazz Singer*, is made; Philo T. Farnsworth invents a vacuum tube called the image dissector and sends the first electronic television picture
1928	The first mechanical TVs go on sale to the public; Farnsworth demonstrates the first working all-electronic television system
1930	Farnsworth receives a patent for his image dissector
1934	The first black-and-white electronic televisions go on sale in Germany
1936	The first electronic televisions go on sale in the UK; the BBC's first live program, *Here's Looking at You*, is broadcast
1938	Vladimir Zworykin receives a patent for his iconoscope; black-and-white electronic televisions go on sale in the United States
1939	Many people see electronic television for the first time at the New York World's Fair
1939–1945	Television production stops during World War II
1950	The first remote control goes on sale; it is attached to the television by a long wire
1953	The first color TVs go on sale
1956	The first wireless remote control becomes available
1969	More than half a billion people tune in to watch the moon landing on television
1971	Closed-captioning is first displayed at the National Conference on Television for the Hearing Impaired in Tennessee
1980	Closed-captioning becomes available on TV channels in the United States
2009	The United States switches to digital television; TVs become available in high-definition and in flat screen.
2014	Samsung launches the largest home television—a 110-inch (279-cm) wide screen model

GLOSSARY

analog (AN-uh-lawg)—the opposite of digital; pictures on an analog TV are made from dots and lines

broadcast (BRAWD-cast)—to send out a program on TV or radio

data (DAY-tuh)—information or facts

digital (DI-juh-tuhl)—the opposite of analog; using binary numbers (0s and 1s) in a form that can be used on a computer or television

engineer (en-juh-NEER)—one who uses science and math to design and build things

lunar module (LOO-nuhr MAH-jool)—the self-contained part of the larger spacecraft that landed on the moon

patent (PAT-uhnt)—a legal document giving sole rights to make or sell a product

receiver (ri-SEE-vur)—a device that receives radio signals and turns them into sound or pictures

signal (SIG-nuhl)—a radio, sound, or light wave that sends information from one place to another

stream (STREEM)—to watch or listen to video or music at the same time that it is being downloaded to your device from the Internet

technology (tek-NOL-uh-jee)—the use of science to do practical things, such as designing complex machines

vacuum tube (VAK-yoom TOOB)—a glass tube that was used in the past in computers and televisions to control the flow of electricity

variety show (vuh-RYE-i-tee SHOH)—a show with many different types of performers, such as dancers, singers, and comedians

wireless message (WIRE-lis MESS-ij)—a telegraph message sent over a long distance using radio waves instead of wires

CRITICAL THINKING QUESTIONS

1. Before television was invented, people entertained themselves in a number of different ways. In what ways has television changed entertainment, for better or worse?

2. Choose two televisions from the book, one early and one modern. Using the text and photos, compare and contrast the two televisions. How has the modern television changed from the early one?

3. In 1969, around half a billion people tuned in to watch American astronauts land on the moon. Using evidence from the Internet and other sources, what recent events have attracted huge amounts of TV viewers?

READ MORE

Enz, Tammy. *The Terrific Tale of Television Technology*. Max Axiom STEM Adventures. North Mankato, Minn.: Capstone Press, 2014.

Hamby, Rachel. *Televisions*. How It Works. Cambridge, Mass.: Focus Readers, 2017.

Laine, Carolee. *Inventing the Television*. Spark of Invention. North Mankato, Minn: Child's World, 2016.

Wyckoff, Edwin Brit. *The Man Who Invented Television: The Genius of Philo T. Farnsworth*. Genius Inventors and Their Great Ideas. Berkeley Heights, N.J.: Enslow Elementary, 2014.

INTERNET SITES

Use FactHound to find Internet sites related to this book.

Visit www.facthound.com

Just type in 9781515798446 and go.

Check out projects, games and lots more at
www.capstonekids.com

INDEX